W9-CLI-880

SLIDE GUITAR CLASSICS

15 Great Songs
featuring the music of:

THE ALLMAN BROTHERS BAND

RY COODER

RORY GALLAGHER

GOV'T MULE

GUNS N' ROSES

Howlin' Wolf with Eric Clapton

LED ZEPPELIN

LITTLE FEAT

BONNIE RAITT

THE ROLLING STONES

TESLA

JOE SATRIANI

JOE WALSH

JOHNNY WINTER

ISBN 1-57560-504-X

Visit our website at www.cherrylane.com

SLIDE GUITAR CLASSICS

4 BIG BAD MOON — JOE SATRIANI

14 Bullfrog Blues — Rory Gallagher

29 Dallas — Johnny Winter

37 Fat Man in the Bathtub — Little Feat

46 The Garden — Guns N' Roses

56 Heaven's Trail (No Way Out) — Tesla

62 Life's Been Good — Joe Walsh

72 Little Red Rooster — Howlin' Wolf with Eric Clapton

81 LITTLE SISTER — RY COODER

91 Mule — Gov't Mule

100 Rock and Roll Doctor — Little Feat

109 Thing Called Love — Bonnie Raitt
(Are You Ready for This Thing Called Love)

117 Trouble No More (Someday Baby) — The Allman Brothers Band

127 Tumbling Dice — The Rolling Stones

134 You Shook Me — Led Zeppelin

BIG BAD MOON

Words and Music by
Joe Satriani

*Trill performed by tapping w/edge of pick.

w/Rhy. Fig. 2 (2 times)

2nd Verse
w/Rhy. Fig. 3 (8 times) & Fill 1

see it now,_ the moon is high_ a - bove._ (w/echo repeats) It's got a

hold on me,_ but I just can't get _ e - nough._ (w/echo repeats)

Big, round, black and_ white,_ I feel the pull, I see _ the light.
w/ad lib vocal

Big bad moon's look - ing down on me to - night._ (w/echo repeats)

(Half time feel)
Chorus

Gtr. I

w/Fill 2
N.C.

Gtr.III
(w/slide)

(Spoken) But I like it.

sl.

don't
pick

steady gliss.

*Above pickups.

Gtr.II

Harm.
(8va)

Harm.
(15ma)

**2
1

tremolo bar

Harm.

Harm.
(15ma)

**2
1

**Pull bar up.

sl.

Rhy. Fig. 3

E5 G5 A5

P.M. P.M. P.M. P.M.

P

Fill 1

sl.

sl.

Fill 2
(Gtr. IV)

Harm.
(15ma)
3½ 1

Harm.
3½ 1

7

9

*Tap w/edge of pick.

w/Rhy. Fig. 1 (2 times)

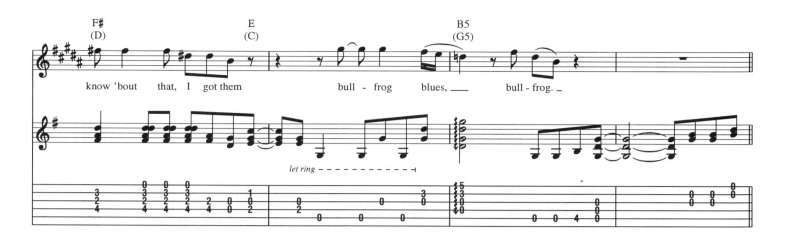

know 'bout that, I got them   bull - frog   blues, ___ bull - frog. _

Guitar Solo

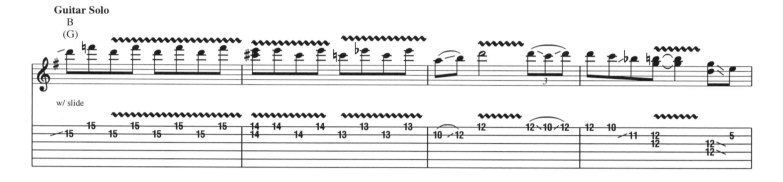

w/ slide

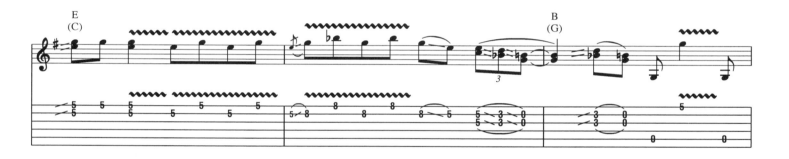

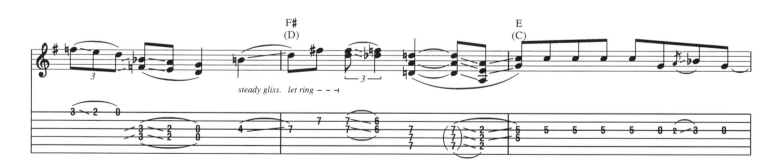

steady gliss.   let ring - - ⌐

17

* Slide positioned halfway between 4th & 5th frets.

Verse

4. My moth-er got __ 'em, my fa-ther got __ 'em,

my sis-ter got __ 'em, my broth-er got 'em. I woke __ up this morn - ing,

19

looked in-side his bag ___ and said, ___ "Well, well." ___

* Gtr. vol. backed-off

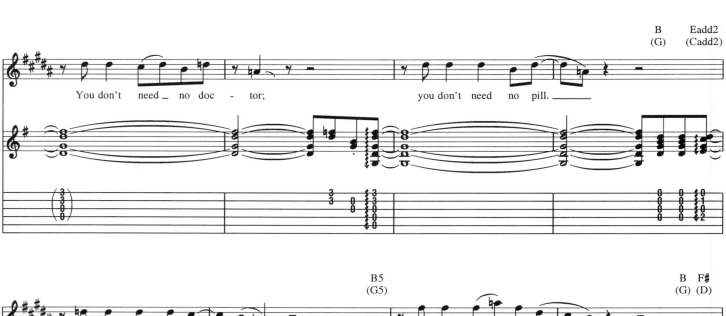

You don't need ___ no doc - tor; you don't need ___ no pill. ___

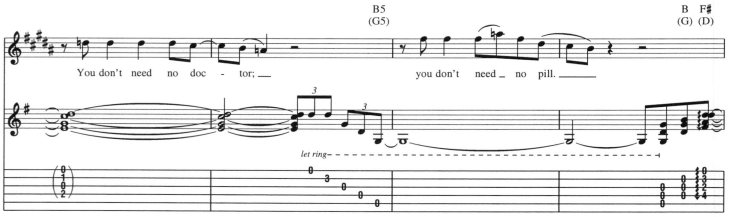

You don't need ___ no doc - tor; ___ you don't need ___ no pill. ___

let ring –

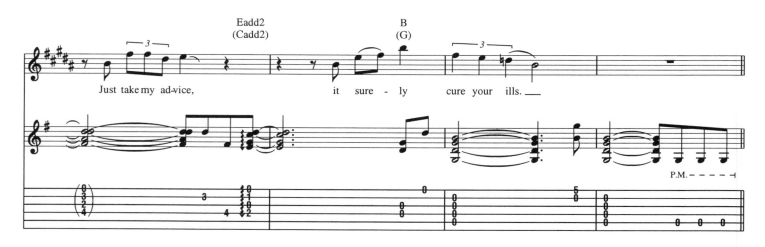

Just take me my ad-vice, it sure - ly cure your ills. ___

P.M. – – – – –

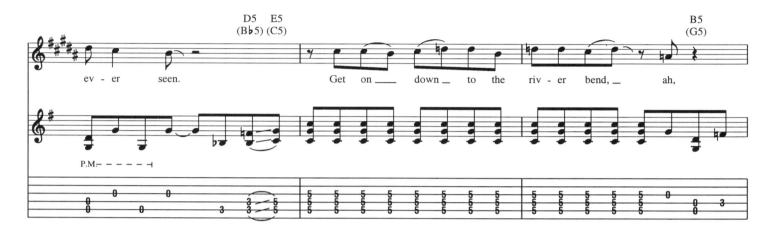

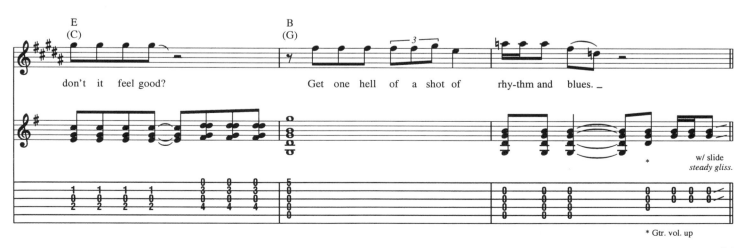

Guitar Solo

** Slide positioned halfway between 15th & 16th frets.

* even

w/o slide

w/ slide

22

steady gliss.

E
(C)

let ring

B
(G)

F#
(D)

E
(C)

let ring

let ring

Verse

B
(G)

N.C.

B5
(G5)

7. Go on down to New ___ Or - leans,

let ring

mp *

w/o slide
let ring

* Gtr. vol. backed-off

$Esus_2^4$
$(Csus_2^4)$

B5
(G5)

the great-est place you've ev - er been.

Head on ___ down to the riv - er bend,___

let ring

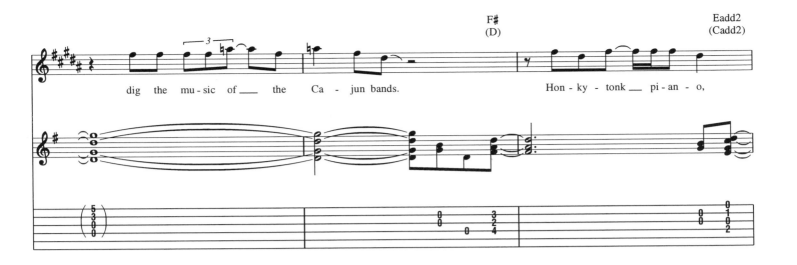

dig the mu-sic of ___ the Ca - jun bands.   Hon - ky - tonk ___ pi - an - o,

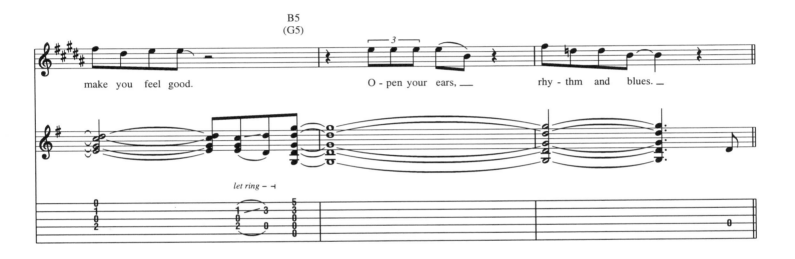

make you feel good.   O - pen your ears, ___   rhy - thm and blues. ___

let ring ⌐

Interlude

N.C.(B)
(N.C.(G))

P.M.— — — — — — ┐   P.M.— — — — — — — — — — — ┐

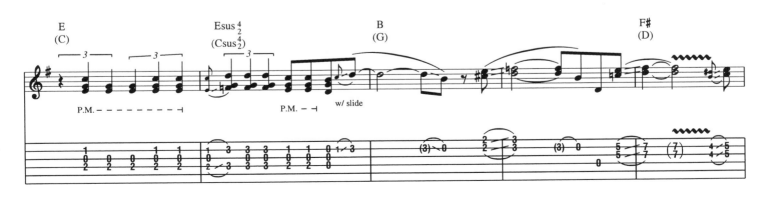

P.M.— — — — — — ┐   P.M.— ┐   w/ slide

26

sit there _ laugh - in',   laugh - in' just to keep from   cry - ing,   one more. _

Guitar Solo

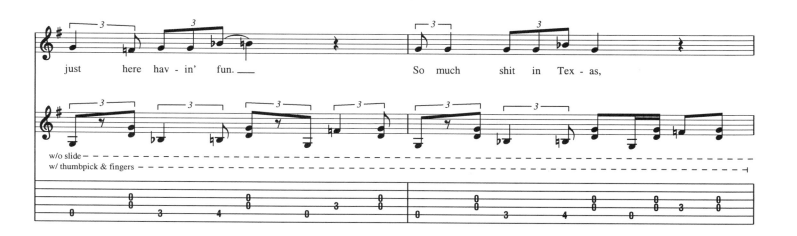

just here hav-in' fun. ___ So much shit in Tex-as,

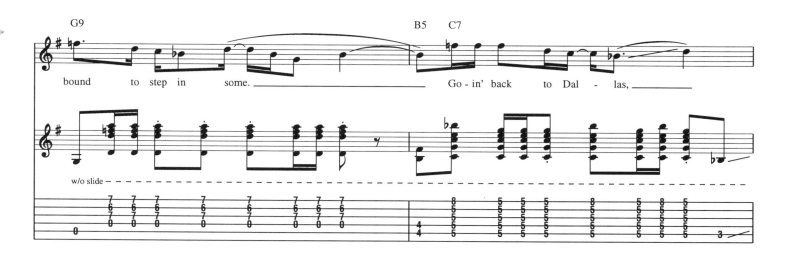

G9   B5 C7

bound to step in some. _____ Go - in' back to Dal - las, _____

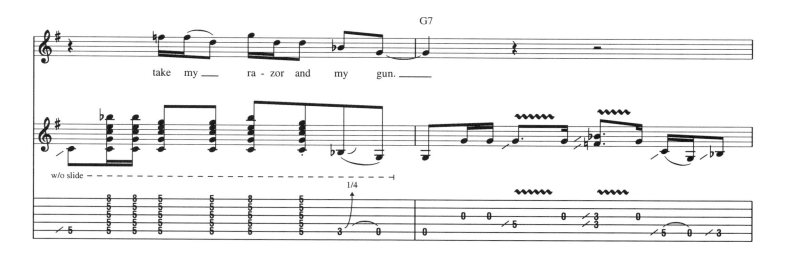

           G7

take my ___ ra - zor and my gun. ___

Man, if peo-ple there are look-in' for trou - ble, _____ yee, _____ sure gon' _____ give 'em _____

Guitar Solo

some.

35

Man, if peo-ple there are look-in' for trou-ble,   yee, ___ sure gon' give 'em ___

some.   Ah, ___ ah. ___

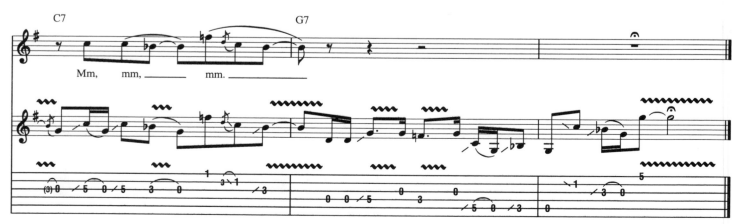

Mm,   mm, ___   mm.

FAT MAN IN THE BATHTUB

Words and Music by
Lowell George

"Hey, ___ mom - ma, hey, ___ let me check your ___ oil, ___ all ___ right?" And she ___ said,

"No, ___ no, ___ hon-ey, ___ not to - night. ___ Come back

Mon - day, ___ yeah, ___ come back Tues - day ___ and

then I ___ might."

fat man _____ in the bath - tub _____ with the blues,

To Coda ⊕

oh, _____ whoa. _____ 'Cause I hear __ you moan, _____ I hear you moan, __

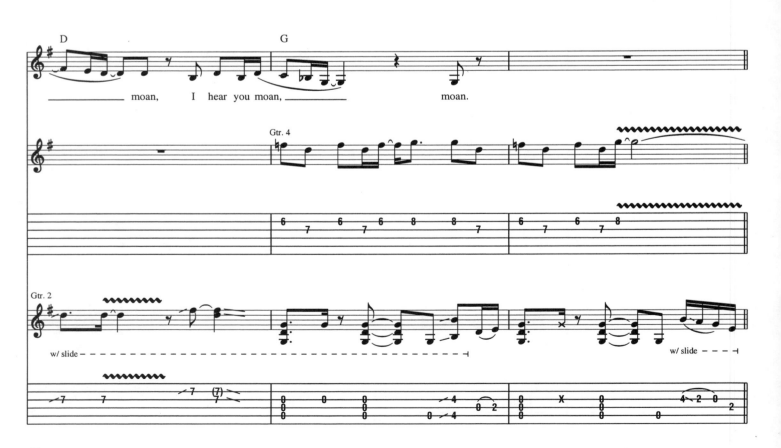

_____ moan, I hear you moan, _____ moan.

THE GARDEN

Words and Music by
West Arkeen, Del James
and Axl Rose

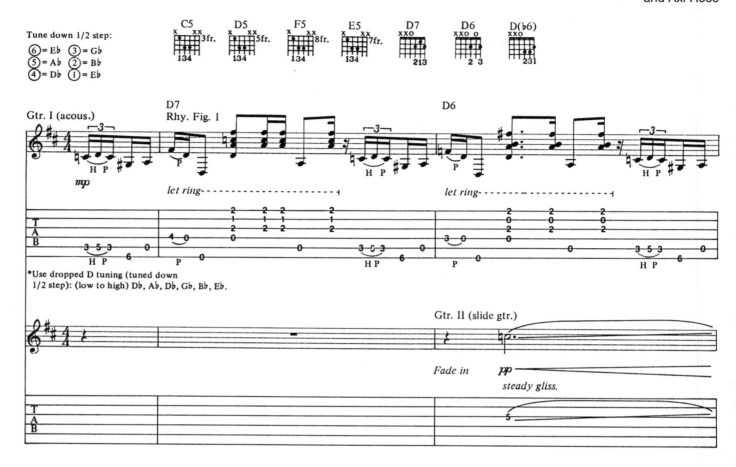

*Use dropped D tuning (tuned down
1/2 step): (low to high) Db, Ab, Db, Gb, Bb, Eb.

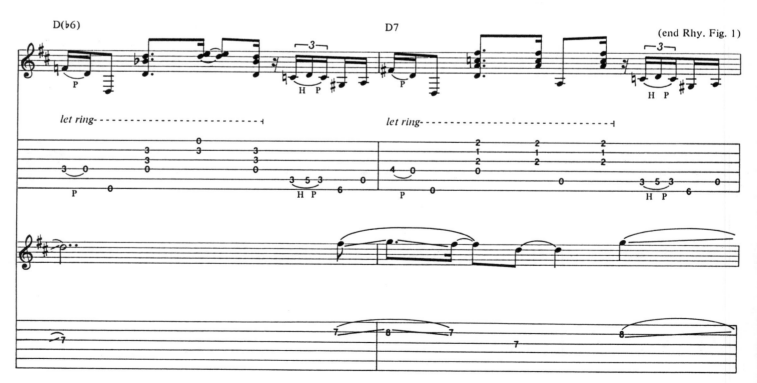

49

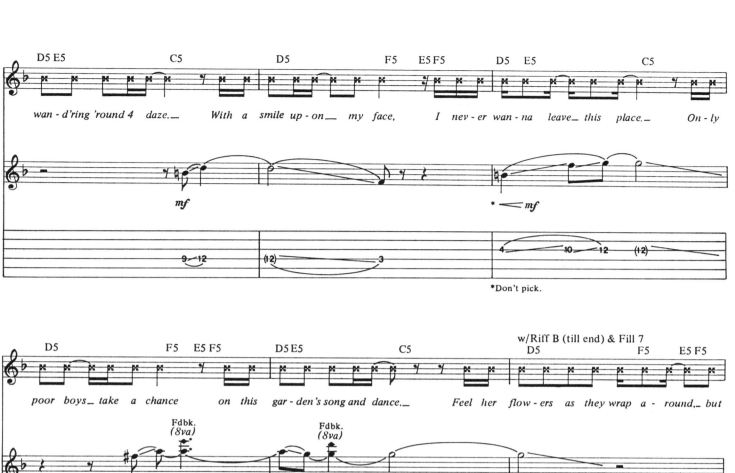

*Don't pick.

Fdbk. pitch: E   D

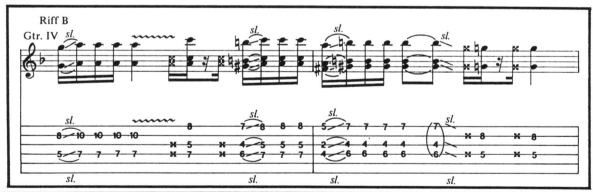

on - ly smart boys do with - out. Turned in - to my__ worst pho - bi - a, it's a cra - zy man's__ u - to - pi - a. If you're

lost no one can show ya, but it sure was glad to know__ ya. Bye, bye._____ So long._____ Bye,

Riff C

Fill 8

*Strum behind nut.

55

HEAVEN'S TRAIL (NO WAY OUT)

Words and Music by
Jeffrey Keith and Tommy Skeoch

1st Verse
w/Rhy. Fig. 1 (4 times)
N.C.(Dm)

slick trip. I'm al - ways read - y to kick ass.— Up on the stage I'm in a rage. Yes, I'm hav - in' the time—

(Band in)

— of my life.— Yes, in - deed.. What a sweet,— sweet life— it is,— 2. Un - til some—

2nd, 3rd Verses
w/Rhy. Fig. 1 (4 times)
N.C.(Dm)

— lo - co two-bit floo - sie with a Lou - ie Le -strange. Ain't good for noth - in' but trou - ble, they're just two fools liv - in'
3. See additional lyrics.

up to their names.— And now it's start - in' to rain ____ on my pa - rade.

Play 2nd time only
w/Rhy. Fig. 2
D5

③ 2fr.
④ open
Elec.   D5
gtr. II

(You) know there's

Elec. gtr. II

Rhy. Fig. 2 (Rhy. gtrs.)

(end Rhy. Fig. 2)

w/Rhy. Fig. 2

⑥ 3fr. ⑥ open
F 1/4 D

noth - in' like the real ___ world ___ to get me down.

w/Rhy. Fig. 2
⑤ 5fr.
D

w/Rhy. Fill 2
Fdbk.
(8va)

sl.

Noth - in' like the world out - side that turns me

57

*w/slide

*Gtr. V solo ad lib -

D.S. al Coda

*Play random noises above 22nd fret with slide.

Coda

w/Rhy. Fig. 3A (1st bar only)   w/Fill 3   w/Rhy. Fig. 3

I guess I'll live in hell.___   There's no way out, no way out

Gtr. V

w/Slide

Additional Lyrics

3. You know I had it made in the shade
Thinkin' that it's not so bad after all.
That's when I woke up, smelled the coffee.
Now I'm back where I started again, yes.
And now it's pourin' rain on my parade.
You know there's nothin' like the real world
To get me down. No!
One is there to lift you up,
One to drag you down.
Now, don't you see
That we're headin' down a one-way, dead-end street. *(To Chorus)*

LIFE'S BEEN GOOD

Words and Music by
Joe Walsh

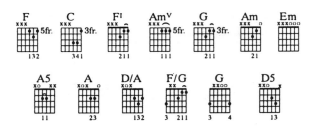

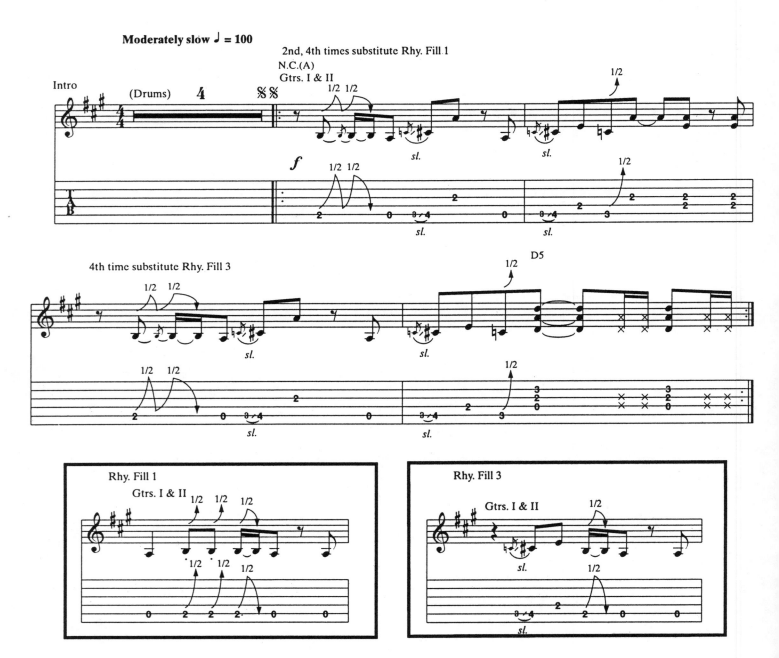

good   to   me ___   so   far. _____

Yeah, ___   yeah,   yeah. ___

Additional Lyrics

3. I make hit records. My fans, they can't wait.
They write me letters, tell me I'm great.
So I got me an office, gold records on the wall.
Just leave a message. Maybe I'll call. *(To 2nd Chorus)*

2nd Chorus:
Lucky I'm sane after all I've been through.
Everybody say I'm cool. (He's cool.)
I can't complain, but sometimes I still do.
Life's been good to me so far.

4. I go to parties, sometimes until four.
It's hard to leave when you can't find the door.
It's tough to handle this fortune and fame.
Everybody's so different. I haven't changed. *(To 3rd Chorus)*

3rd Chorus:
They say I'm lazy, but it takes all my time.
Everybody says, "Oh, yeah." (Oh, yeah.)
I keep on going. Guess I'll never know why.
Life's been good to me so far.

LITTLE RED ROOSTER

Written by Willie Dixon

Moderately slow ♩ = 78

Triplet feel (♫ = ♪♪)

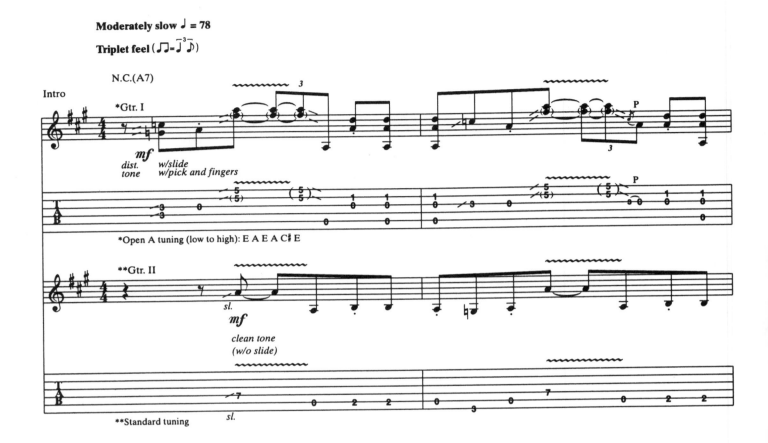

*Open A tuning (low to high): E A E A C♯ E

**Standard tuning

little red roost-er,   too la-zy to crow to-day.

Keeps ev-'ry-thing in the barn-yard   up-set in ev-'ry way.

74

Oh, watch out all— you kin-folk,

lit-tle red— roost-er's on the prowl.—

Guitar solo
w/Rhy. Fig. 1
N.C.(A7)

trem. pick

76

78

LITTLE SISTER

Words and Music by
Doc Pomus and Mort Shuman

*Tune all gtrs. to open G (⑥ = D, ⑤ = G, ④ = D, ③ = G, ② = B, ① = D) and capo at 3rd fret.
**All notes tabbed at 3rd fret are to be played as open stgs.

84

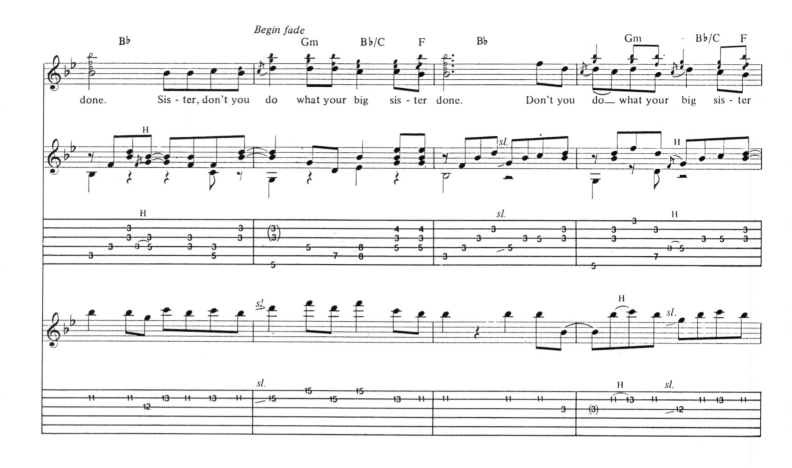

MULE

Written by Warren Haynes,
Allen Woody and Matthew Abts

N.C.(E5)

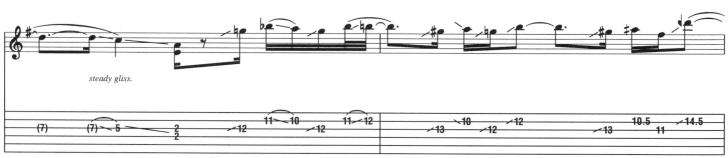

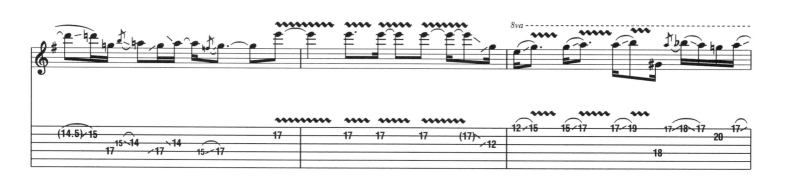

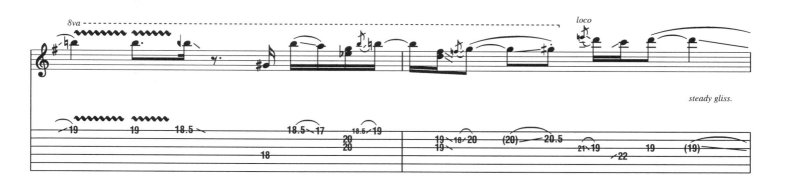

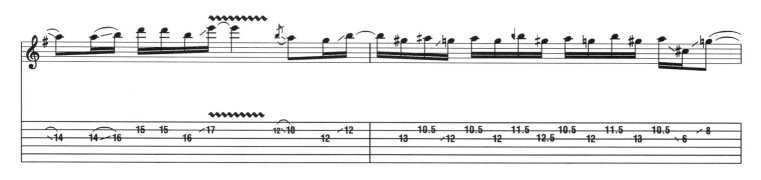

97

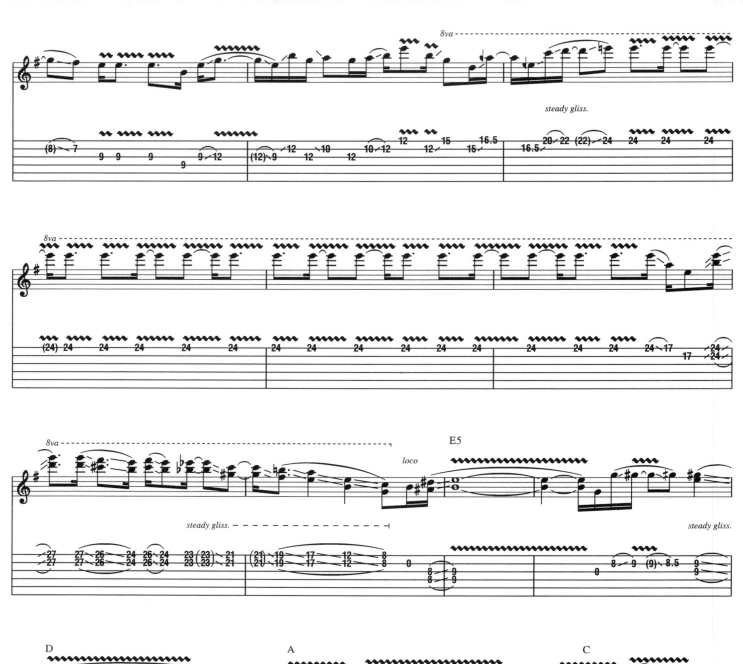
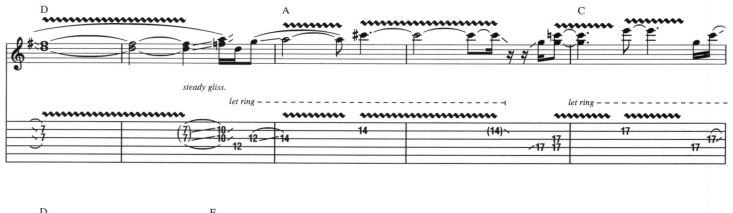
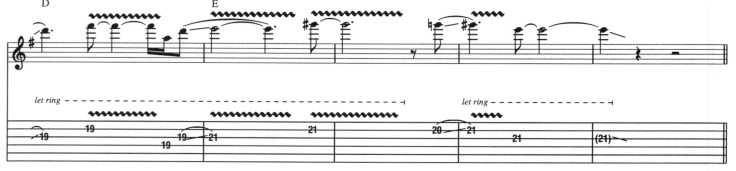

Breakdown

Gtr. 1 tacet
N.C.(E5)

Where's my mule? Where's my for-ty a-cres? _____ Where's my dream, Mis-ter E -

man-ci-pa-tor? _____ Live this ___ way, might as well

meet my mak-er. _____ Where's my, my, my, my, my mule? _

Outro

Em7

2nd & 3rd times, Gtr. 1: w/ Fill 1

Gtr. 1

Play 3 times

w/o slide

Em7

mp

Fill 1
Gtr. 1

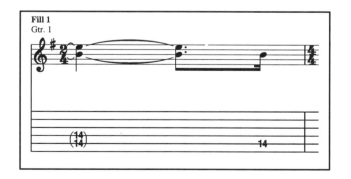

ROCK AND ROLL DOCTOR

Words and Music by
Lowell George and Martin Kibbee

Gtr. 2 tuning:
(low to high) E–A–D–G–B–D

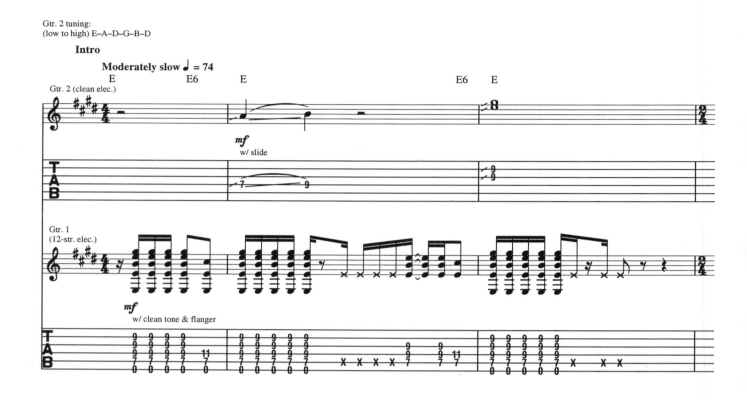

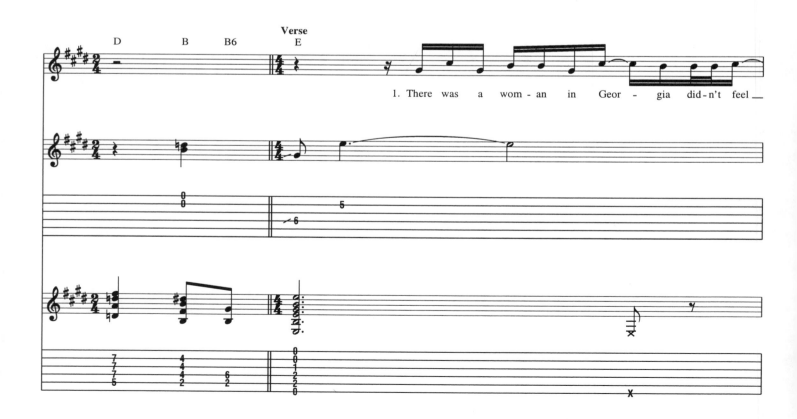

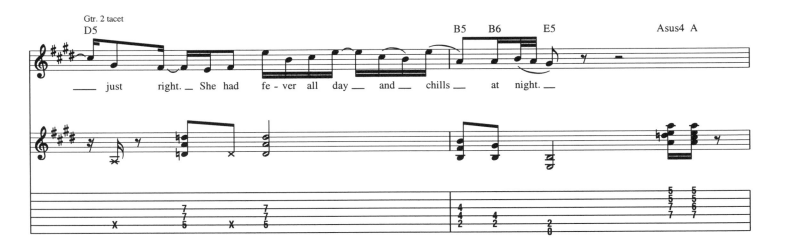

just right. She had fe - ver all day _ and _ chills _ at night. _

Now, _ things got _ worse, yes, a se - ri - ous bind. _ At times like this _ it takes a

man with such style _ like you not of - ten find. _ A doc - tor of the heart and a doc - tor of the mind. _____

ask   the rock and roll   doc - tor's ad - vice. _____   2. It's

Verse

just   a   coun-try town   but the   pa-tients   come __   from Mo-bile   to   Mo-line,   from miles   a - round, __

3. Two de-grees in be-bop, a P-h.-D. in swing, he's a mas-ter of rhy-thm, he's a rock

and roll   king, __ yeah. ____   Mm _ hmm. _____   If

Chorus

you like   coun-try with a boog-ie   beat __ he's   the   man   to meet. _   Mm,
(Uh, he's the man   to   meet.) ___

mm.   If you like the sound of shuf-flin' feet _ he can't _ be beat. _   Mm,
(I say he can't be beat.) _

oh _ yeah.   If you,   if you wan-na,   if you wan-na feel _ real nice, _ just

A   D   B   E   N.C.(E)

ask   the rock and roll   doc - tor's ad - vice.

THING CALLED LOVE
(Are You Ready for This Thing Called Love)

Words and Music by
John Hiatt

*Pull slide back from 3rd fr. to mid-point between 3rd & 2nd frets. Sounding pitch is E one quarter-tone flat.

Don't have to hum-ble your-self to me.___ I ain't your judge or your king.___

___ Ba - by, you know I ain't no Queen of

110

114

TROUBLE NO MORE
(Someday Baby)

Written by
McKinley Morganfield (Muddy Waters)

* A Dorian

(D5)

A5

It's good, kind   treat - ment, ___   bring you home some ___ day.
Oh, with - out my   lov - in' yeah, ___   oh, you can't stay ___ long.
I don't want no   wom-an no, ___   who can't have no ___ man.

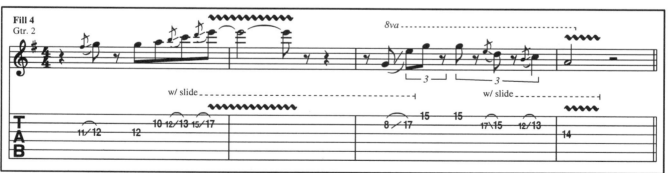

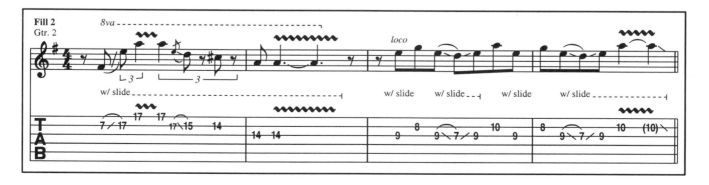

Gtr. 2: w/ Fill 3, 2nd time; w/ Fill 6, 3rd time

Some day   ba - by,   you ain't gon-na trou - ble ____   poor ____ me ____   an - y
But some day   ba - by,   you ain't gon-na trou - ble ____   poor ____ me ____   an - y
But some day   ba - by,   you ain't gon-na trou - ble ____   poor ____ me ____   an - y

End Rhy. Fig. 1

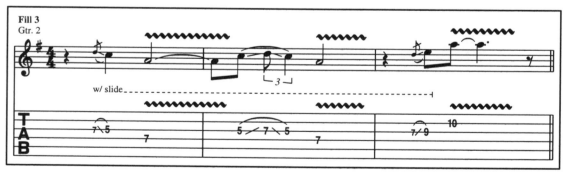

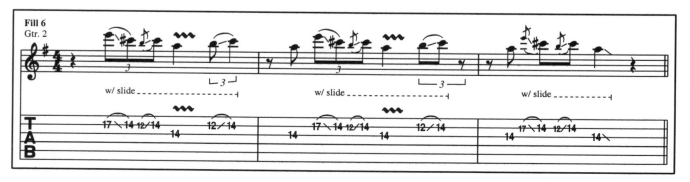

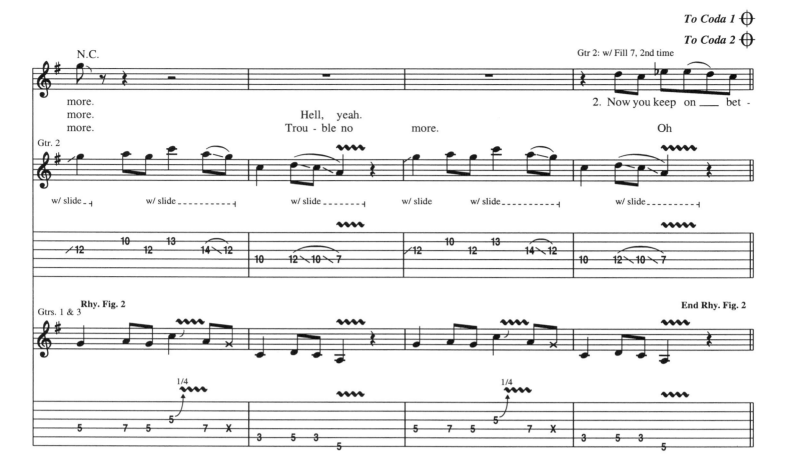

To Coda 1
To Coda 2

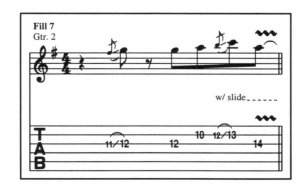

but you don't _ do me no _____ good _

But some day ba - by, _____ you ain't gon-na

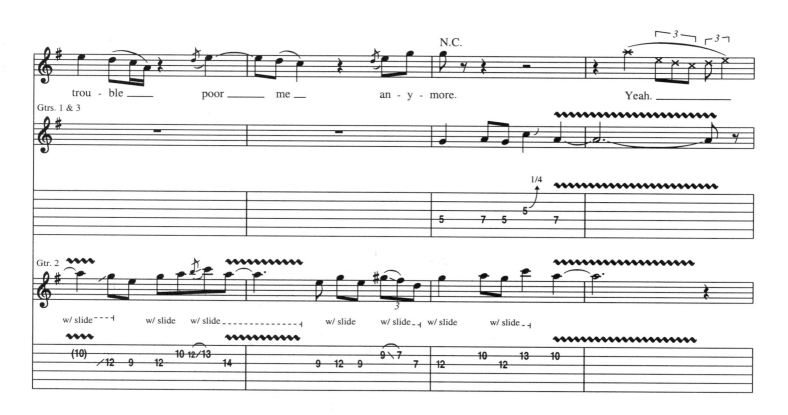

trou - ble _____ poor _____ me _ an - y - more.

Yeah. _____

Gtrs. 1 & 3

Gtr. 2

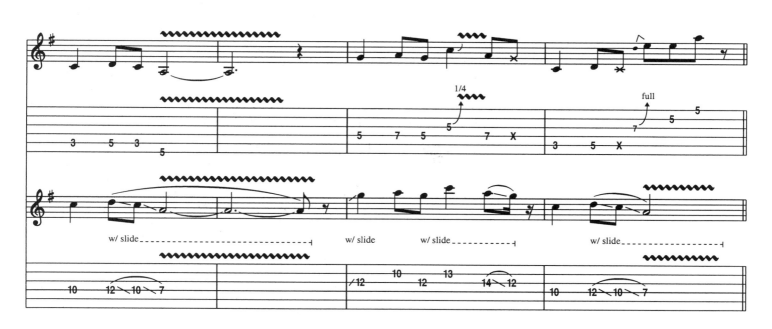

Guitar Solo

Gtr. 3: w/ Rhy. Fig. 1

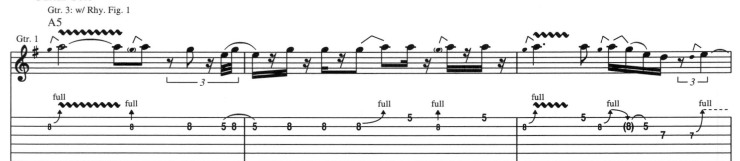

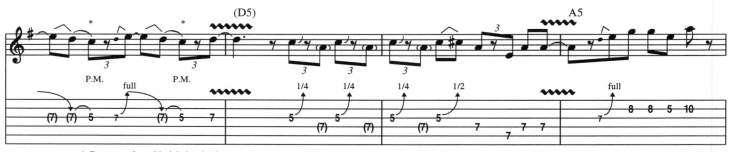

* Dampen string with right hand palm
as you pull off from previous note.

D.S. al Coda 1

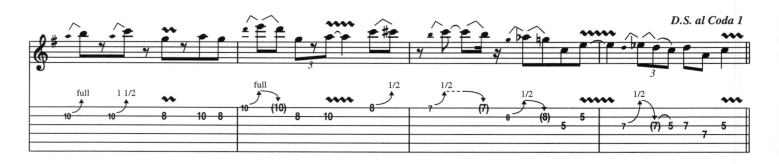

⊕ *Coda 1*
Guitar Solo

Gtr. 3: w/ Rhy. Fig. 1

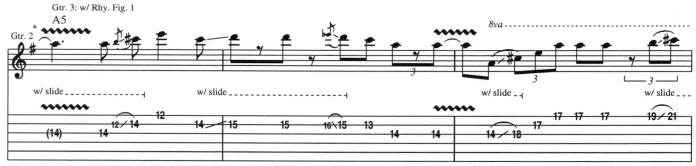

* continued from Fill 7

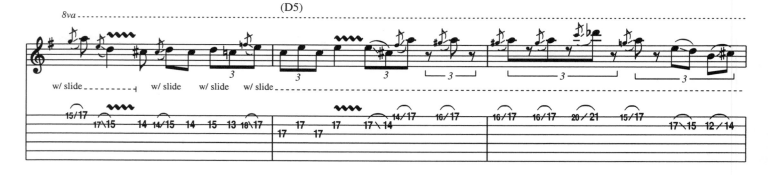

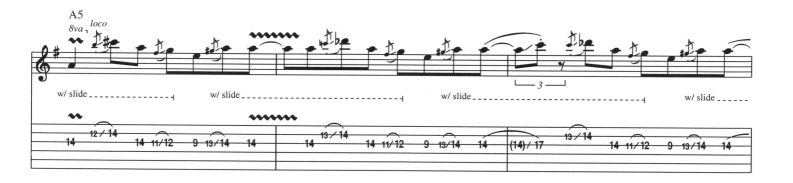

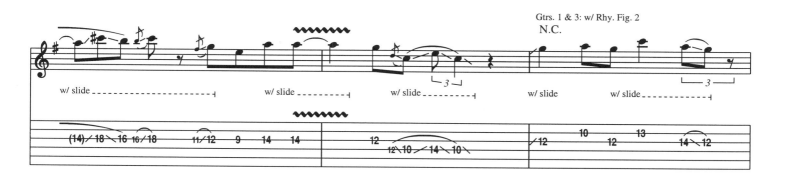

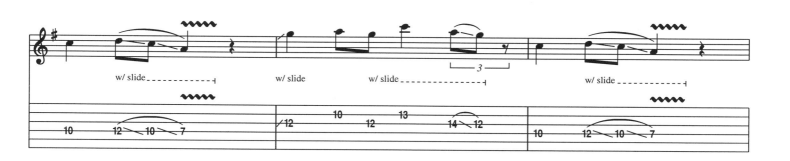

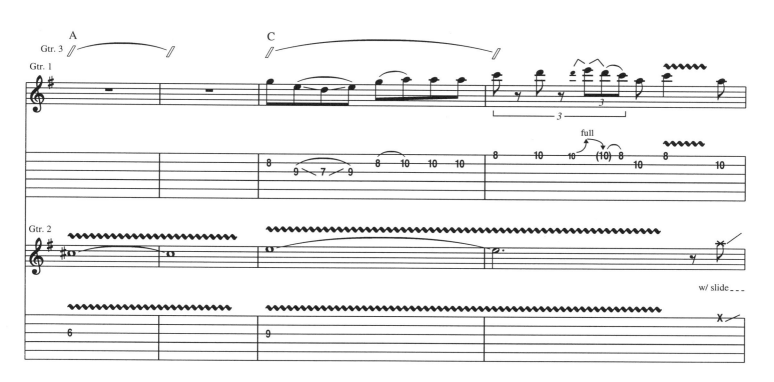

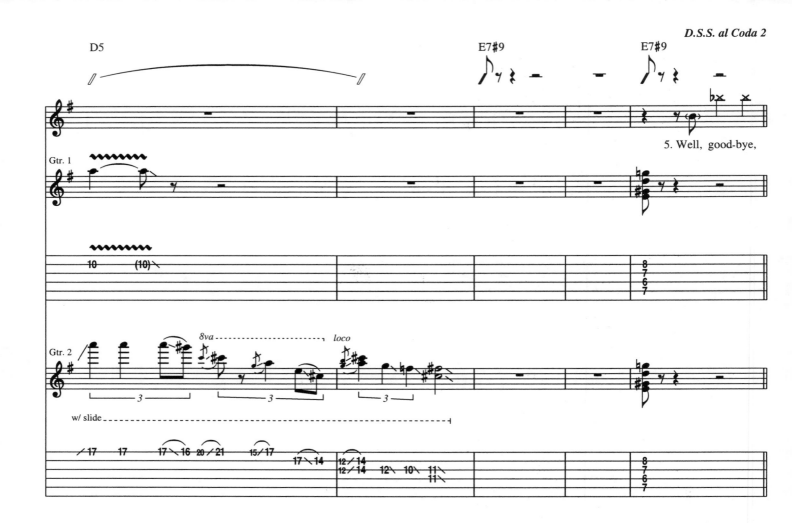

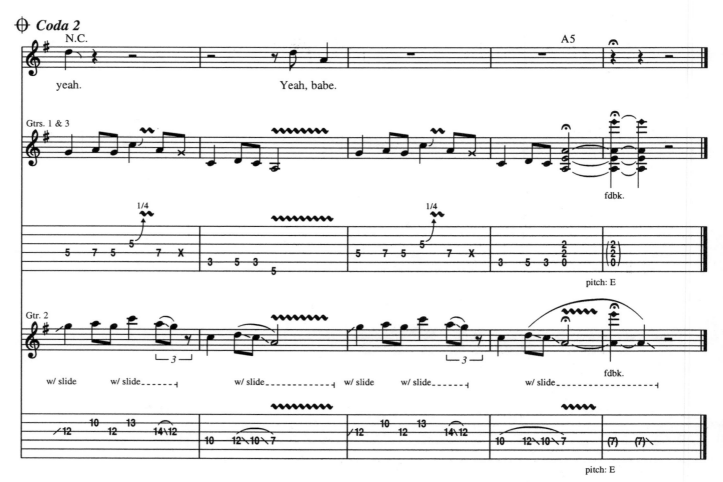

mon - ey. I'm all six - es and sev - ens and nines.___ Say___

(end Riff B)

5th Verse
w/Rhy. Figs. 1 & 2 and Fill 2 (Gtr. II)   w/Riff B (last 5 bars only)(Gtr. II)

___ now, ba - by, I'm the rank out - sid - er.   You   can be my part - ner in crime.___

w/Rhy. Fig. 3 (1st 2 bars only)(Gtrs. I & III)
F♯   B   F♯   B

_____   But ba - by,   I   can't   stay.   You got to

w/Rhy. Fill 3 (Gtrs. I & III)
N.C.(E)   w/Rhy. Fill 5 (Gtr. I & III)

roll _____ me   and call me the tum - bl - in'...   Roll _____ me   and

w/Rhy. Fills 1 (Gtr. I) & 3 (Gtr. III)
B

call me the tum - bl - in'   dice._____

Gtr. II   sl.   1/2

sl.   w/o slide
1/2

Fill 2 (Gtr. II)

w/slide

131

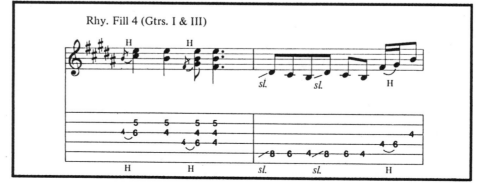

YOU SHOOK ME

Written by
Willie Dixon and J.B. Lenoir

*Key signature denotes E Dorian.

**Chord symbols reflect overall tonality.

1. You know you shook me, —

2., 3. *See Additional Lyrics*

you shook me all — night long. _____

You know you shook —

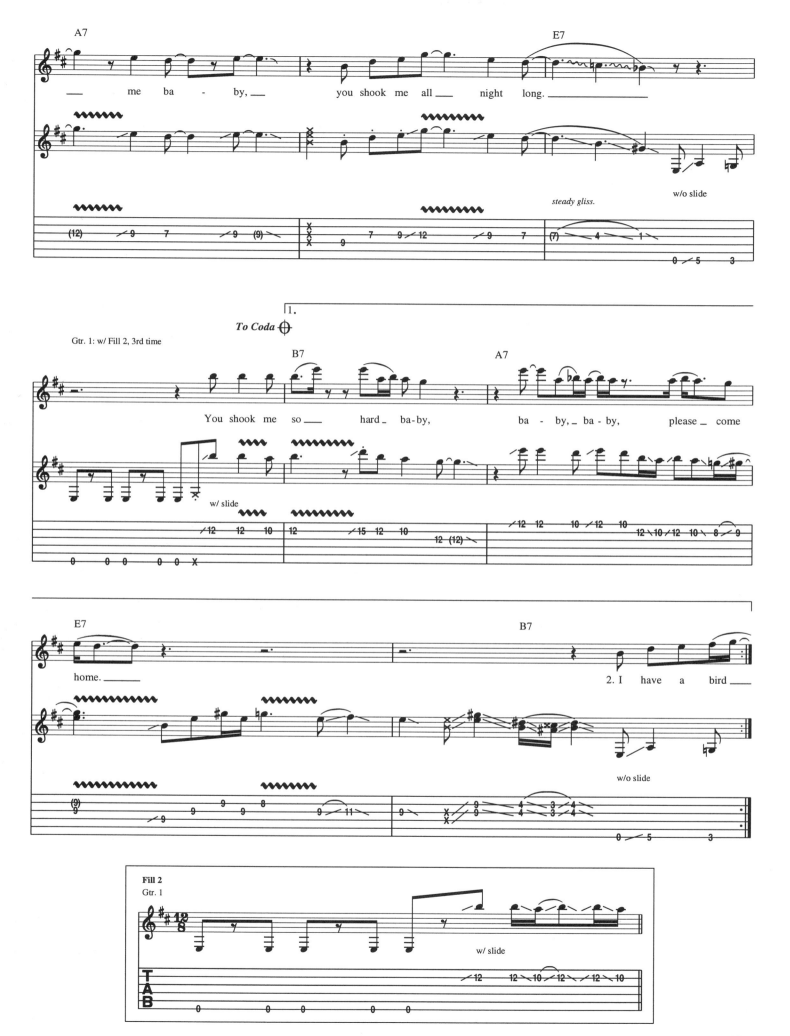

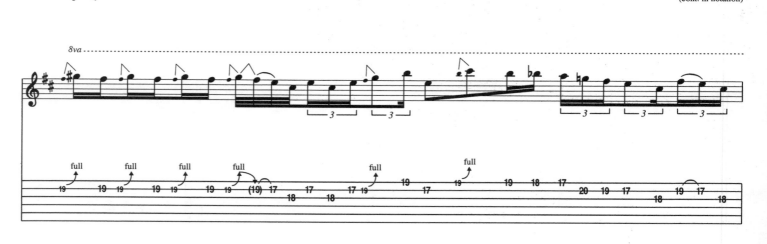

(cont. in notation)

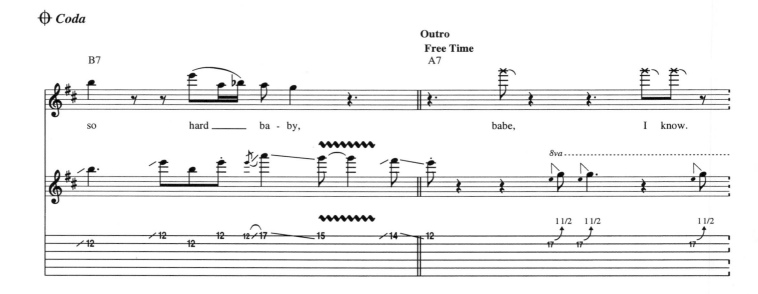

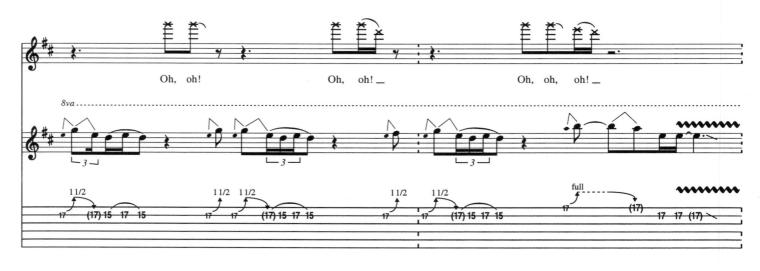

140

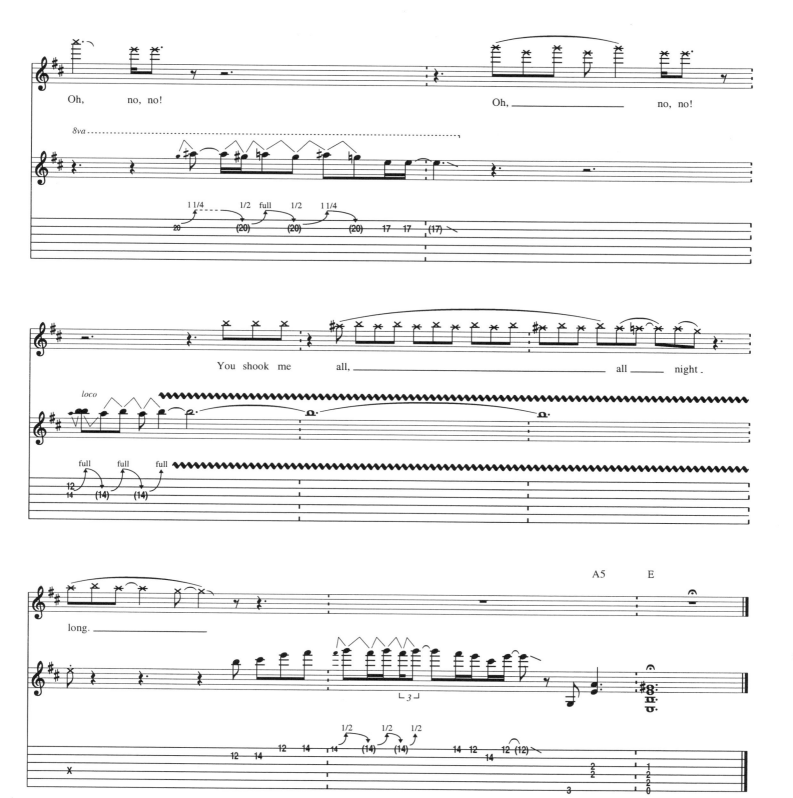

Additional Lyrics

2. I have a bird that whistles and
   I have birds that sing.
   I have a bird that whistles and
   I have birds that sing.
   I have a bird won't do nothin; oh, oh, oh, oh,
   without a diamond ring.

3. You know you shook me, babe,
   You shook me all night long.
   I know you really, really did, babe.
   I think you shook me, baby,
   You shook me all night long.
   You shook me so hard, baby, I know.

Guitar Notation Legend

Guitar Music can be notated three different ways: on a *musical staff*, in *tablature*, and in *rhythm slashes*.

RHYTHM SLASHES are written above the staff. Strum chords in the rhythm indicated. Use the chord diagrams found at the top of the first page of the transcription for the appropriate chord voicings. Round noteheads indicate single notes.

THE MUSICAL STAFF shows pitches and rhythms and is divided by bar lines into measures. Pitches are named after the first seven letters of the alphabet.

TABLATURE graphically represents the guitar fingerboard. Each horizontal line represents a string, and each number represents a fret.

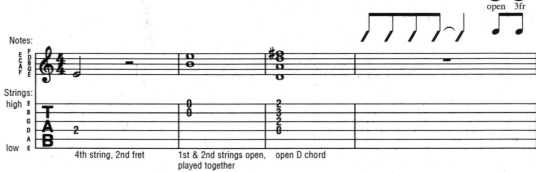

4th string, 2nd fret   1st & 2nd strings open, played together   open D chord

HALF-STEP BEND: Strike the note and bend up 1/2 step.

BEND AND RELEASE: Strike the note and bend up as indicated, then release back to the original note. Only the first note is struck.

HAMMER-ON: Strike the first (lower) note with one finger, then sound the higher note (on the same string) with another finger by fretting it without picking.

TRILL: Very rapidly alternate between the notes indicated by continuously hammering on and pulling off.

PICK SCRAPE: The edge of the pick is rubbed down (or up) the string, producing a scratchy sound.

TREMOLO PICKING: The note is picked as rapidly and continuously as possible.

WHOLE-STEP BEND: Strike the note and bend up one step.

PRE-BEND: Bend the note as indicated, then strike it.

PULL-OFF: Place both fingers on the notes to be sounded. Strike the first note and without picking, pull the finger off to sound the second (lower) note.

TAPPING: Hammer ("tap") the fret indicated with the pick-hand index or middle finger and pull off to the note fretted by the fret hand.

MUFFLED STRINGS: A percussive sound is produced by laying the fret hand across the string(s) without depressing, and striking them with the pick hand.

VIBRATO BAR DIVE AND RETURN: The pitch of the note or chord is dropped a specified number of steps (in rhythm) then returned to the original pitch.

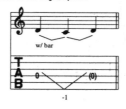

GRACE NOTE BEND: Strike the note and immediately bend up as indicated.

VIBRATO: The string is vibrated by rapidly bending and releasing the note with the fretting hand.

LEGATO SLIDE: Strike the first note and then slide the same fret-hand finger up or down to the second note. The second note is not struck.

NATURAL HARMONIC: Strike the note while the fret-hand lightly touches the string directly over the fret indicated.

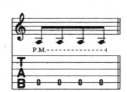

PALM MUTING: The note is partially muted by the pick hand lightly touching the string(s) just before the bridge.

VIBRATO BAR SCOOP: Depress the bar just before striking the note, then quickly release the bar.

SLIGHT (MICROTONE) BEND: Strike the note and bend up 1/4 step.

WIDE VIBRATO: The pitch is varied to a greater degree by vibrating with the fretting hand.

SHIFT SLIDE: Same as legato slide, except the second note is struck.

PINCH HARMONIC: The note is fretted normally and a harmonic is produced by adding the edge of the thumb or the tip of the index finger of the pick hand to the normal pick attack.

RAKE: Drag the pick across the strings indicated with a single motion.

VIBRATO BAR DIP: Strike the note and then immediately drop a specified number of steps, then release back to the original pitch.

CHERRY LANE MUSIC COMPANY

6 East 32nd Street, New York, NY 10016

Quality in Printed Music

The Magazine You Can Play

Visit the Guitar One web site at **www.guitarone.com**

ACOUSTIC INSTRUMENTALISTS
INCLUDES TAB

Over 15 transcriptions from legendary artists such as Leo Kottke, John Fahey, Jorma Kaukonen, Chet Atkins, Adrian Legg, Jeff Beck, and more.

02500399 Play-It-Like-It-Is Guitar $9.95

THE BEST BASS LINES
INCLUDES TAB

24 super songs: Bohemian Rhapsody • Celebrity Skin • Crash Into Me • Crazy Train • Glycerine • Money • November Rain • Smoke on the Water • Sweet Child O' Mine • What Would You Say • You're My Flavor • and more.

02500311 Play-It-Like-It-Is Bass $14.95

BLUES TAB
INCLUDES TAB

14 songs: Boom Boom • Cold Shot • Hide Away • I Can't Quit You Baby • I'm Your Hoochie Coochie Man • In 2 Deep • It Hurts Me Too • Talk to Your Daughter • The Thrill Is Gone • and more.

02500410 Play-It-Like-It-Is Guitar $14.95

CLASSIC ROCK TAB
INCLUDES TAB

15 rock hits: Cat Scratch Fever • Crazy Train • Day Tripper • Hey Joe • Hot Blooded • Start Me Up • We Will Rock You • You Really Got Me • and more.

02500408 Play-It-Like-It-Is Guitar $14.95

MODERN ROCK TAB
INCLUDES TAB

15 of modern rock's best: Are You Gonna Go My Way • Denial • Hanging by a Moment • I Did It • My Hero • Nobody's Real • Rock the Party (Off the Hook) • Shock the Monkey • Slide • Spit It Out • and more.

02500409 Play-It-Like-It-Is Guitar $14.95

SIGNATURE SONGS
INCLUDES TAB

21 artists' trademark hits: Crazy Train (Ozzy Osbourne) • My Generation (The Who) • Smooth (Santana) • Sunshine of Your Love (Cream) • Walk This Way (Aerosmith) • Welcome to the Jungle (Guns N' Roses) • What Would You Say (Dave Matthews Band) • and more.

02500303 Play-It-Like-It-Is Guitar $16.95

BASS SECRETS

WHERE TODAY'S BASS STYLISTS GET TO THE BOTTOM LINE
compiled by John Stix

Bass Secrets brings together 48 columns highlighting specific topics – ranging from the technical to the philosophical – from masters such as Stu Hamm, Randy Coven, Tony Franklin and Billy Sheehan. They cover topics including tapping, walking bass lines, soloing, hand positions, harmonics and more. Clearly illustrated with musical examples.

02500100 ....$12.95

CLASSICS ILLUSTRATED

WHERE BACH MEETS ROCK
by Robert Phillips

Classics Illustrated is designed to demonstrate for readers and players the links between rock and classical music. Each of the 30 columns from *Guitar* highlights one musical concept and provides clear examples in both styles of music. This cool book lets you study moving bass lines over stationary chords in the music of Bach and Guns N' Roses, learn the similarities between "Leyenda" and "Diary of a Madman," and much more!

02500101 ....$9.95

GUITAR SECRETS
INCLUDES TAB

WHERE ROCK'S GUITAR MASTERS SHARE THEIR TRICKS, TIPS & TECHNIQUES
compiled by John Stix

This unique and informative compilation features 42 columns culled from *Guitar* magazine. Readers will discover dozens of techniques and playing tips, and gain practical advice and words of wisdom from guitar masters.

02500099 ....$10.95

IN THE LISTENING ROOM

WHERE ARTISTS CRITIQUE THE MUSIC OF THEIR PEERS
compiled by John Stix

A compilation of 75 columns from *Guitar* magazine, *In the Listening Room* provides a unique opportunity for readers to hear major recording artists remark on the music of their peers. These artists were given no information about what they would hear, and their comments often tell as much about themselves as they do about the music they listened to. Includes candid critiques by music legends like Aerosmith, Jeff Beck, Jack Bruce, Dimebag Darrell, Buddy Guy, Kirk Hammett, Eric Johnson, John McLaughlin, Dave Navarro, Carlos Santana, Joe Satriani, Stevie Ray Vaughan, and many others.

02500097 ....$14.95

LEGENDS OF LEAD GUITAR

THE BEST OF INTERVIEWS: 1995-2000

This is a fascinating compilation of interviews with today's greatest guitarists! From deeply rooted blues giants to the most fearless pioneers, legendary players reveal how they achieve their extraordinary craft.

02500329 ....$14.95

LESSON LAB

This exceptional book/CD pack features more than 20 in-depth lessons. Tackle in detail a variety of pertinent music- and guitar-related subjects, such as scales, chords, theory, guitar technique, songwriting, and much more!

02500330 Book/CD Pack $19.95

NOISE & FEEDBACK

THE BEST OF 1995-2000: YOUR QUESTIONS ANSWERED

If you ever wanted to know about a specific guitar lick, trick, technique or effect, this book/CD pack is for you! It features over 70 lessons on composing • computer assistance • education and career advice • equipment • technique • terminology and notation • tunings • and more.

02500328 Book/CD Pack $17.95

OPEN EARS

A JOURNEY THROUGH LIFE WITH GUITAR IN HAND
by Steve Morse

In this collection of 50 *Guitar* magazine columns from the mid-'90s on, guitarist Steve Morse sets the story straight about what being a working musician *really* means. He deals out practical advice on: playing with the band, songwriting, recording and equipment, and more, through anecdotes of his hard-knock lessons learned.

02500333 ....$10.95

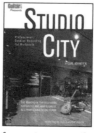

SPOTLIGHT ON STYLE

THE BEST OF 1995-2000: AN EXPLORER'S GUIDE TO GUITAR

This book and CD cover 18 of the world's most popular guitar styles, including: blues guitar • classical guitar • country guitar • funk guitar • jazz guitar • Latin guitar • metal • rockabilly and more!

02500320 Book/CD Pack $19.95

STUDIO CITY

PROFESSIONAL SESSION RECORDING FOR GUITARISTS
by Carl Verheyen

In this collection of colomns from Guitar Magazine, guitarists will learn how to: exercise studio etiquette and act professionally • acquire, assemble and set up gear for sessions • use the tricks of the trade to become a studio hero • get repeat call-backs • and more.

02500195 ....$9.95

THE HOTTEST TAB SONGBOOKS AVAILABLE FOR GUITAR & BASS!

PLAY IT LIKE IT IS GUITAR
WITH TABLATURE

NOTE-FOR-NOTE TRANSCRIPTIONS

PLAY IT LIKE IT IS BASS
WITH TABLATURE

NOTE-FOR-NOTE TRANSCRIPTIONS

from **CHERRY LANE MUSIC COMPANY**

Quality in Printed Music

Guitar Transcriptions

02500443	Alien Ant Farm – ANThology	$19.95
02500009	Bush – Best of	$19.95
02501272	Bush – 16 Stone	$21.95
02501288	Bush – Razorblade Suitcase	$21.95
02500193	Bush – The Science of Things	$19.95
02500098	Coal Chamber	$19.95
02500174	Coal Chamber – Chamber Music	$19.95
02500179	Mary Chapin Carpenter – Authentic Guitar Style of	$16.95
02501257	Faith No More – King for a Day/ Fool for a Lifetime	$19.95
02500132	Evolution of Fear Factory	$19.95
02500198	Best of Foreigner	$19.95
02501242	Guns N' Roses – Anthology	$24.95
02506953	Guns N' Roses – Appetite for Destruction	$22.95
02501286	Guns N' Roses Complete, Volume 1	$24.95
02501287	Guns N' Roses Complete, Volume 2	$24.95
02506211	Guns N' Roses – 5 of the Best, Vol. 1	$12.95
02506975	Guns N' Roses – GN'R Lies	$19.95
02500299	Guns N' Roses – Live Era '87-'93 Highlights	$24.95
02501193	Guns N' Roses – Use Your Illusion I	$24.95
02501194	Guns N' Roses – Use Your Illusion II	$24.95
02500387	Best of Heart	$19.95
02500007	Hole – Celebrity Skin	$19.95
02501260	Hole – Live Through This	$19.95
02500024	Best of Lenny Kravitz	$19.95
02500380	Lenny Kravitz – Greatest Hits	$19.95
02500375	Lifehouse – No Name Face	$19.95
02500362	Best of Little Feat	$19.95
02501259	Machine Head – Burn My Eyes	$19.95
02500173	Machine Head – The Burning Red	$19.95

02500305	Best of The Marshall Tucker Band	$19.95
02501357	Dave Matthews Band – Before These Crowded Streets	$19.95
02501279	Dave Matthews Band – Crash	$19.95
02500389	Dave Matthews Band – Everyday	$19.95
02501266	Dave Matthews Band – Under the Table and Dreaming	$19.95
02500131	Dave Matthews/Tim Reynolds – Live at Luther College	$19.95
02501195	Metallica – Metallica	$22.95
02506965	Metallica – ...And Justice for All	$22.95
02500070	Metallica – Garage Inc.	$24.95
02507018	Metallica – Kill 'Em All	$19.95
02501232	Metallica – Live: Binge & Purge	$19.95
02501275	Metallica – Load	$24.95
02507920	Metallica – Master of Puppets	$19.95
02501297	Metallica – Reload	$24.95
02507019	Metallica – Ride the Lightning	$19.95
02500279	Metallica – S&M Highlights	$24.95
02506210	Metallica – 5 of the Best/Vol.1	$12.95
02506235	Metallica – 5 of the Best/Vol. 2	$12.95
02501353	Best of Steve Morse	$19.95
02500348	Ozzy Osbourne – Blizzard of Ozz	$19.95
02501277	Ozzy Osbourne – Diary of a Madman	$19.95
02509973	Ozzy Osbourne – Songbook	$24.95
02507904	Ozzy Osbourne/Randy Rhoads Tribute	$22.95
02500316	Papa Roach – Infest	$19.95
02500194	Powerman 5000 – Tonight the Stars Revolt!	$17.95
02500025	Primus Anthology – A-N (Guitar/Bass)	$19.95
02500091	Primus Anthology – O-Z (Guitar/Bass)	$19.95
02501255	Best of Joe Satriani	$19.95
02501268	Joe Satriani	$22.95
02501299	Joe Satriani – Crystal Planet	$24.95
02500306	Joe Satriani – Engines of Creation	$22.95
02501205	Joe Satriani – The Extremist	$22.95

02506236	Joe Satriani – 5 of the Best/Vol. 2	$12.95
02507029	Joe Satriani – Flying in a Blue Dream	$22.95
02507074	Joe Satriani – Not of This Earth	$19.95
02506959	Joe Satriani – Surfing with the Alien	$19.95
02501226	Joe Satriani – Time Machine 1	$19.95
02501227	Joe Satriani – Time Machine 2	$19.95
02500088	Sepultura – Against	$19.95
02501239	Sepultura – Arise	$19.95
02501240	Sepultura – Beneath the Remains	$19.95
02501238	Sepultura – Chaos A.D.	$19.95
02501241	Sepultura – Schizophrenia	$19.95
02500188	Best of the Brian Setzer Orchestra	$19.95
02500177	Sevendust	$19.95
02500176	Sevendust – Home	$19.95
02500090	Soulfly	$19.95
02501250	Best of Soundgarden	$19.95
02501230	Soundgarden – Superunknown	$19.95
02500167	Best of Steely Dan for Guitar	$19.95
02500168	Steely Dan's Greatest Songs	$19.95
02501263	Tesla – Time's Making Changes	$19.95
02500199	Best of Zakk Wylde	$22.95

Bass Transcriptions

02500008	Best of Bush	$16.95
02505920	Bush – 16 Stone	$19.95
02506966	Guns N' Roses – Appetite for Destruction	$19.95
02500013	Best of The Dave Matthews Band	$16.95
02505911	Metallica – Metallica	$19.95
02506982	Metallica – ...And Justice for All	$19.95
02500075	Metallica – Garage, Inc.	$24.95
02507039	Metallica – Kill 'Em All	$19.95
02505919	Metallica – Load	$19.95
02506961	Metallica – Master of Puppets	$19.95
02505926	Metallica – Reload	$21.95
02507040	Metallica – Ride the Lightning	$17.95
02500288	Metallica – S&M Highlights	$19.95
02505925	Ozzy Osbourne – Diary of a Madman	$17.95
02500025	Primus Anthology – A-N (Guitar/Bass)	$19.95
02500091	Primus Anthology – O-Z (Guitar/Bass)	$19.95
02505918	Best of Sepultura for Bass	$18.95
02505917	Best of Soundgarden	$16.95

FOR MORE INFORMATION, SEE YOUR LOCAL MUSIC DEALER, OR WRITE TO:

HAL•LEONARD® CORPORATION

7777 W. BLUEMOUND RD. P.O. BOX 13819 MILWAUKEE, WI 53213

Prices, contents and availability subject to change without notice.